COUTURE
CUPCAKES

ERIC LANLARD & PATRICK COX

MITCHELL BEAZLEY

An Hachette UK Company
www.hachette.co.uk

First published as *Cox Cookies & Cake*
in Great Britain in 2011 by Mitchell Beazley,
an imprint of Octopus Publishing Group Ltd,
Endeavour House, 189 Shaftesbury Avenue,
London WC2H 8JY
www.octopusbooks.co.uk

This abridged edition published in 2014

British Library Cataloguing-in-Publication Data.
A catalogue record for this book is available
from the British Library.

Commissioning editor Becca Spry
Senior Editor Sybella Stephens
Home Economist Rachel Wood
Senior Art Editor Juliette Norsworthy
Designer Jaz Bahra
Photography Patrick Llewelyn-Davies
Production Controller Allison Gonsalves

ISBN: 978 1 84533 934 0
Printed and bound in China
10 9 8 7 6 5 4 3 2 1

All recipes have been tested in metric.
Muffin-size cupcake tins and standard
muffin paper cases should be used for all
cupcake recipes, unless otherwise stated.
Medium eggs and full fat milk should be
used, unless otherwise stated.

CONTENTS

I'm a designer. It's in my blood. It's who I am. It affects how I look at everything in the world. I see everyday objects, such as shoes, bags or cakes, and I want to make them sexier, inject them with glamour and make them shine! For me life is the triumph of the fantastic over the dull, and when I saw the pastel-shaded world of cupcakes, I wanted to shake it up, sex it up and create something breathtakingly new.

The result was our Cox Cookies & Cake project – a bakery we opened in Soho. The location was a former sex shop in the heart of London's historic red light district; with an original Tracey Emin neon piece on the wall; staff in leather-studded aprons; mirrored ceilings and a polished black floor – it all set the scene for the most dangerous thing to hit the world of cupcakes since self-raising flour.

However, when it came to the cakes themselves, I faced my limitations as a designer. I needed a skilled pâtissier and business partner to make sure the cakes tasted every bit as good as they looked, with all the quality that one associates with the Patrick Cox name. Fortunately Elizabeth Hurley introduced me to world-renowned and fabulous Eric Lanlard (he made Elizabeth's wedding cake) and as soon as we met I knew instantly we could work together. We created cakes that were sexy, unbelievably tasty and fun. Each cake was like a work of art.

This book takes that accessibility further. I want people to enjoy the design process themselves and have fun creating these cakes at home. So turn on the music, crank up the volume and get baking!

Patrick Cox

I'm a pâtissier. It's in my blood and who I am, or at least who I have been since I was a little boy staring in the windows of my local pâtisserie. In times where form often triumphs over substance and where looks too often succeed over taste, it has always been my mission to make cakes that taste as good as they look; cakes where the feasting of the eyes is not followed by a bite of disappointment, but by a feasting of the taste buds. I have been putting this philosophy into practice within my own business over the past 18 years.

Before having the pleasure of meeting Patrick, glamour was always very much part of my world, reflected in the title of my first book *Glamour Cakes* and my first two TV series' *Glamour Puds*. As an artisan I've always used cake design as my creative outlet. However, the excitement I felt on first hearing about Patrick's vision, pushed my boundaries way beyond anything I would have dared to do myself.

The results of our efforts speak for themselves in this book. I hope these recipes enable you to bake a little excitement in your own home and put happy faces on your friends and family alike.

Eric Lanlard

NUTTY
& CHOCOLATE
CUPCAKES

COLA CUPCAKES

Put some fizz into your cupcakes! These little miracles will delight kids and adults, too. The cola makes the cake light and airy, and the addition of the popping candy topping makes them a truly fun experience.

MAKES 12 CUPCAKES

200g (7oz) unsalted butter
200ml (7fl oz) cola (I prefer to use the old-fashioned original one as it has more flavour)
250g (8oz) self-raising flour
1 tsp baking powder
1 tbsp cocoa powder
2 eggs, beaten
150ml (¼ pint) milk

For the cola frosting
100g (3½oz) unsalted butter, softened
25g (1oz) cocoa powder
450g (14½oz) icing sugar
100ml (3½fl oz) cola
1 tsp vanilla extract
cola-flavoured popping candy or fizzy cola bottles, to decorate

Preheat the oven to 200°C/fan 180°C/gas mark 6, and line a cupcake tin with paper cases.

In a saucepan, gently heat the butter and cola until the butter has melted. Remove from the heat and leave to cool.

Sift the flour, baking powder and cocoa together. Add the cooled cola and butter mix, followed by the eggs and milk. Mix together until smooth.

Divide the mixture between the paper cases. Bake for 25–30 minutes, or until a skewer inserted into a cupcake comes out clean. Leave to cool in the tin for 5 minutes then transfer to a wire rack and allow to cool completely before frosting.

To make the Cola Frosting: Cream the butter in a bowl. Sift the cocoa and icing sugar together and mix into the butter a little at a time, alternating with additions of the cola. Beat to give a nice smooth frosting. (You may need to add more cola if the frosting is too stiff). Beat in the vanilla extract.

Pipe the frosting on the cooled cupcakes and decorate with either popping candy or cola bottles.

RED VELVET CUPCAKES

This now celebrated cupcake is usually made as a large cake and there are many variations, including some that use beetroot juice to give the rich red colour. In this recipe I use a combination of pure cocoa, vinegar and red food colouring to achieve a vibrant tone.

MAKES 12 CUPCAKES

30g (1¼oz) cocoa powder
1 tsp vanilla extract
75g (3oz) unsalted butter, softened
175g (6oz) caster sugar
2 egg yolks
pinch of salt
150ml (¼ pint) buttermilk
150g (5oz) plain flour, sifted
½ tsp bicarbonate of soda
½ tsp white wine vinegar
1 tsp red food colouring

For the frosting
125ml (4fl oz) milk
1½ tbsp flour
pinch of salt
100g (3½oz) unsalted butter, softened
175g (6oz) icing sugar, plus extra for dusting
100g (3½oz) white chocolate, melted and cooled
½ tsp vanilla extract

Preheat the oven to 200°C/fan 180°C/gas mark 6, and line a cupcake tin with paper cases.
....
In a small bowl, mix the cocoa and vanilla extract together and set aside.
....
In a large bowl, beat the butter and sugar together using a free-standing mixer or an electric hand whisk set on a medium-high speed. Add the egg yolks and beat for one more minute. Add the cocoa and vanilla to the mixture.
....
Stir the salt into the buttermilk, mix one-third into the mixture, followed by one-third of the flour. Repeat with two further batches of each until all are mixed in.
....
Mix the bicarbonate of soda with the vinegar and blend this and the food colouring into the batter. Divide the mixture between the paper cases and bake for 20–25 minutes, or until a skewer inserted into the centre of a cupcake comes out clean.
....
Allow the cupcakes to cool in the tin for 10 minutes. Then remove the cupcakes from the tin and allow to cool completely before frosting.
....
To make the frosting: in a small saucepan, whisk the milk, flour and salt over a medium heat for 1 or 2 minutes until the mixture thickens and begins to bubble. Transfer to a small bowl and leave to cool.
....
Beat the butter and icing sugar together until light and fluffy. Add the cooled chocolate, the milk mixture and the vanilla extract, and mix until smooth and fluffy.
....
Spread the frosting or pipe it on to the cooled cakes, and finish by crumbling some cooked red sponge on the top (you may have to sacrifice one of your cakes) and dust with icing sugar.

TRIPLE CHOCOLATE CUPCAKES

This is one for the chocoholics! There's cocoa, melted chocolate and chocolate chips in this beautiful moist cupcake. Then, for a rich finish, it's topped with chocolate frosting and chocolate sprinkles. Heaven!

MAKES 12 CUPCAKES

75g (3oz) dark chocolate, broken into pieces
200g (7oz) unsalted butter
225g (7½oz) caster sugar
3 eggs
½ tsp baking powder
175g (6oz) plain flour
25g (1oz) cocoa powder
50g (2oz) dark chocolate chips
1 quantity Chocolate Frosting (see page 87)
mixture of mini white, milk and dark chocolate sprinkles, to decorate

Preheat the oven to 200°C/fan 180°C/gas mark 6, and line a cupcake tin with paper cases.

In a large saucepan, melt the chocolate and butter over medium heat, stirring to prevent burning. Allow this to cool for a few minutes.

Stir in the sugar until well mixed. Add the eggs, one at a time, until you have a smooth batter. Sift the baking powder, flour and cocoa into the batter and mix until smooth. Fold in the chocolate chips.

Divide the mixture between the paper cases, but don't over-fill them, just about three-quarters full. Bake for 20–25 minutes, or until a skewer inserted into the centre of a cupcake comes out clean.

Leave to cool in the tins for 5 minutes then transfer to a wire rack and allow to cool completely before frosting. I like to top these with Chocolate Frosting and cover with mini chocolate sprinkles to decorate.

IRISH CREAM
& CHOCOLATE CUPCAKES

We call this classic the Irish cupcake because of the addition of Irish cream liqueur, which works perfectly with the chocolate base. Kids should be kept well away from these!

MAKES 12 CUPCAKES

75g (3oz) dark chocolate,
    plus extra for decorating
200g (7oz) unsalted butter
225g (7½oz) caster sugar
1 tsp vanilla extract
1 tbsp of Irish cream liqueur
3 eggs
25g (1oz) cocoa powder
175g (6oz) plain flour
½ tsp baking powder
chocolate curls, to decorate

For the frosting
225g (7½oz) unsalted butter
75g (3oz) dark chocolate,
    melted and cooled
550g (1lb 2oz) icing sugar
3 tbsp Irish cream liqueur

Preheat the oven to 200°C/fan 180°C/gas mark 6, and line a cupcake tin with paper cases.

Put the chocolate and butter together in a large heatproof bowl and place over a saucepan of barely simmering water, making sure the bowl does not touch the surface of the water. Stir until completely melted then remove from the heat. Stir in the sugar, vanilla extract and Irish cream liqueur.

Beat in the eggs one at a time. Sift in the cocoa powder, flour and baking powder and mix well until combined and smooth.

Spoon the mixture into the prepared cases, filling each three-quarters full. Bake for 20–25 minutes, or until a skewer inserted into the centre of a cupcake comes out clean.

Leave to cool in the tin for 5 minutes then transfer to a wire rack and allow to cool completely before covering with frosting.

To make the frosting: beat the butter into the melted chocolate until smooth. Gradually beat in the icing sugar and finally add the Irish cream liqueur. Using a small palette knife, spread the frosting over the cupcakes or pipe it on in spirals. Decorate with chocolate curls.

CHOCOLATE & COCONUT CUPCAKES

If you are a fan of the chocolate bar Bounty, these cupcakes are for you. Coated with a rich cinnamon ganache, they have a true taste of paradise.

MAKES 12 CUPCAKES

200g (7oz) caster sugar
200g (7oz) unsalted butter, softened
3 eggs
3 tbsp milk
175g (6oz) self-raising flour
½ tsp baking powder
75g (3oz) desiccated coconut

For the chocolate ganache
150g (5oz) dark chocolate (55% cocoa solids), broken into small pieces
150ml (¼ pint) double cream
50g (2oz) very soft unsalted butter
1 tsp ground cinnamon
toasted desiccated coconut, to decorate

Preheat the oven to 200°C/fan 180°C/gas mark 6, and line a cupcake tin with paper cases.

In a large bowl, cream the sugar and butter together until pale and fluffy using a free-standing mixer or electric hand whisk, then stir in the eggs one at a time, followed by the milk. Beat until everything is well incorporated.

Sift the flour and baking powder and fold them into butter mixture until smooth and well incorporated. Finally fold in the coconut.

Divide the mixture between the paper cases. Bake for 20 minutes or until a skewer inserted into a cupcake comes out clean. Leave to cool in the tin for 5 minutes and then transfer to a wire rack to cool completely.

To make the Chocolate Ganache: place the chocolate in a medium bowl. Put the cream in a small saucepan over a medium heat and, as soon as it reaches boiling point, pour it over the chocolate. Leave this to stand until the chocolate pieces have melted.

Once they are melted, pass the mixture through a sieve. Then stir in the softened butter and cinnamon, and leave to cool and slightly set.

Once the mixture has set use a free-standing mixer or an electric hand whisk, and beat until it has almost doubled in volume.

Spread the ganache over the cooled cupcakes and sprinkle with toasted desiccated coconut to decorate.

CHOCOLATE & RASPBERRY CUPCAKES

The rich dark chocolate cake and the sweetness of the raspberries is a combination made in heaven. Then, topped with chocolate frosting and more fresh raspberries... yum!

MAKES 12 CUPCAKES

125g (4oz) unsalted butter
75g (3oz) dark chocolate, broken into large pieces
1 tsp instant coffee
1 tsp vanilla essence
150g (5oz) light soft brown sugar
2 eggs, lightly beaten
1 tsp baking powder
225g (7½oz) self-raising flour
150ml (¼ pint) water
450g/14oz raspberries, plus extra to decorate
1 quantity Chocolate Frosting (see page 87)

Preheat the oven to 200°C/fan 180°C/gas mark 6, and line a cupcake tin with paper cases.

Melt the butter in a large heatproof bowl placed over a saucepan of barely simmering water, making sure the bowl does not touch the surface of the water. When it is half melted, add the chocolate. When the chocolate is completely melted remove from the heat and stir to mix in any lumps, then allow to cool for a few minutes.

Dissolve the coffee in the vanilla essence, then add this mixture and the brown sugar to the cooled chocolate and butter. When these are fully mixed together, add the eggs and mix in.

Sift the baking powder and the flour into the mixture and beat until all ingredients are well incorporated and the batter is thick. Then stir in the water a little at a time, making sure the liquid is entirely absorbed into the batter.

Divide the mixture between the paper cases, filling each about half full. Place 3 raspberries on the surface of each – they will sink into the batter. Then fill each case almost to the top and place another fresh raspberry on top.

Bake for about 25 minutes, or until each cupcake is firm to touch or a skewer inserted into a cupcake comes out clean. Leave to cool in the tin for 10 minutes and then transfer to a wire rack to cool completely. Once cool, pipe Chocolate Frosting in swirls on top of each cupcake and decorate with fresh raspberries on top.

BLACK FOREST CUPCAKES

Don't be put off by the lengthy preparation needed for this recipe – all the effort is well worth it to make these very tasty grown-up cakes. I like using Amarena cherries if I can get them – Italian delis often stock them.

MAKES 12 CUPCAKES

425g (14oz) jar or can of stoned cherries in syrup, drained (reserving the syrup)
100g (3½oz) dark chocolate (50% cocoa solids), broken into pieces
165g (5½oz) unsalted butter, roughly chopped
300g (10oz) caster sugar
4 tbsp cherry brandy
150g (5oz) plain flour, sifted
2 tbsp self-raising flour, sifted
2 tbsp cocoa powder
1 egg

For the decoration
2 tsp cherry brandy
200ml (7fl oz) whipping cream
50g (2oz) chunk of dark chocolate (50% cocoa solids) optional

Preheat the oven to 200°C/fan 180°C/gas mark 6, and line a cupcake tin with paper cases.

Put 100g (3½oz) of the cherries and 125ml (4fl oz) of their syrup in a food processor and process until it becomes a smooth purée.

Cut the remaining cherries in half and reserve the rest of the syrup.

Place the cherry purée in a saucepan together with the chocolate, butter, sugar and cherry brandy. Stir over a low heat until the chocolate has melted. Pour into a large bowl and allow to cool for 15 minutes.

When cool, whisk in the flours and the cocoa powder, followed by the egg. It will be very runny, but that is OK.

Divide the mixture between the paper cases. You will probably find that you fill the cases close to the top, but do not worry, as the cupcakes will not rise a great deal.

Bake for 40–45 minutes, or until firm to touch or until a skewer inserted into a cupcake comes out clean. Allow to cool in the tin for 5 minutes then transfer to a wire rack to cool completely.

To decorate, mix the cherry brandy into the remaining cherry halves. Whip the cream to soft peaks, and pipe swirls on top of each cake.

Top each cake with some of the brandy-soaked cherry halves and drizzle over the reserved syrup. If using, scrape along the side of the chocolate with a vegetable peeler to create curls and use these to decorate the top of each cake.

CHOCOLATE & MARSHMALLOW CUPCAKES

For this recipe I use a mixture of mini marshmallows and Marshmallow Fluff to top a rich and gooey brownie-like cupcake. If you haven't used Marshmallow Fluff before, seek it out from specialist food halls and American food stores – it gives these little devilish cupcakes a fun, toasted-marshmallow dimension and an extra marshmallow hit!

MAKES 12 CUPCAKES

75g (3oz) dark chocolate, broken into pieces
200g (7oz) unsalted butter
225g (7½oz) caster sugar
3 eggs
½ tsp baking powder
25g (1oz) cocoa powder
175g (6oz) plain flour
icing sugar, to decorate

For the marshmallow buttercream frosting
250g (8oz) unsalted butter, softened
125g (4oz) Marshmallow Fluff, plus extra to decorate
mini marshmallows, to decorate (optional)

Preheat the oven to 200°C/fan 180°C/gas mark 6, and line a cupcake tin with paper cases.

In a large saucepan over medium heat, melt the chocolate and butter, stirring to prevent any burning. Allow to cool for a few minutes, then stir in sugar until well mixed.

Add the eggs, one at a time, until you have a smooth batter. Then sift in the baking powder, flour and cocoa and mix just until smooth.

Divide the mixture between the paper cases filling them about three-quarters full – don't over fill them. Bake for 20–25 minutes or until a skewer inserted into a cupcake comes out clean. Leave to cool in the tin for 10 minutes and then transfer to a wire rack to cool completely.

To make the Marshmallow Buttercream Frosting: Beat the butter and Marshmallow Fluff together until smooth. Using a small palette knife, spread the frosting on top of the cupcakes. If you want to add an extra marshmallow hit, spoon a couple of teaspoons of Fluff on top of the frosting, add some mini marshmallows, if liked, and dust with icing sugar.

Beware! The Fluff will drip down the frosting, so don't let these cakes hang around for too long – although I love the way they look when this happens.

COCONUT CUPCAKES

This recipe uses a very soft coconut sponge with an indulgent mascarpone icing. I like using long strands of dry coconut for the topping. To spoil yourself, try drizzling a bit of melted dark chocolate on top. This recipe can be made very grown-up by the addition of some Malibu coconut liqueur!

MAKES 12 CUPCAKES

175g (6oz) unsalted butter, softened
125g (4oz) caster sugar
3 eggs, beaten
20g (¾oz) cocoa powder
50g (2oz) desiccated coconut
150g (5oz) plain flour
1 tsp baking powder
4 tbsp milk

For the frosting
300g (10oz) mascarpone
50g (2oz) icing sugar
zest of 1 lime
50g (2oz) desiccated coconut
40g (1½oz) thin strands of fresh coconut, toasted

Preheat the oven to 200°C/fan 180°C/gas mark 6, and line a cupcake tin with paper cases.

In a large bowl, cream together the butter and sugar until pale and light. Add the beaten eggs and mix well. Add the cocoa powder and coconut, and mix in well. Mix together the flour, baking powder and then fold into the butter-and-egg mixture. Add the milk and mix until smooth.

Divide the mixture between the paper cases and bake on the middle shelf of the oven for 20 minutes, or until the cakes are golden and a skewer inserted into the centre of a cupcake comes out clean. Leave to cool in the tin for 5 minutes and then transfer to a wire rack to cool completely.

To make the frosting: Mix the mascarpone, icing sugar and lime zest together until smooth. Add the desiccated coconut and mix in well. When ready, spread an even layer of the mascarpone mixture over the top of each cake and sprinkle with toasted coconut.

PISTACHIO & ROSEWATER CUPCAKES

Here are all the Middle Eastern flavours in a cute little cupcake – the combination of the spices, floral essences and nuts works so well. I like to top mine with dried organic rose petals.

MAKES 12 CUPCAKES

125ml (4fl oz) natural yoghurt
160ml (5½fl oz) milk
5 tbsp sunflower oil
175g (6oz) caster sugar
1½ tbsp rosewater
175g (6oz) plain flour
2 tbsp cornflour
½ tsp bicarbonate of soda
½ tsp baking powder
1 tsp vanilla extract
generous pinch of cardamom
  seeds (the little black seeds
  inside cardamom pods)
50g (2oz) chopped pistachios

For the rosewater glaze
200g (7oz) icing sugar
15g (½oz) unsalted butter
2–3 tsp milk
½ tsp rosewater

Preheat the oven to 200°C/fan 180°C/gas mark 6, and line a cupcake tin with paper cases.

In a large bowl, whisk together the yoghurt, milk, oil, sugar and rosewater. Sift in the flour, cornflour, bicarbonate of soda and baking powder, then stir in the vanilla extract, cardamom seeds and chopped pistachios.

Divide the mixture between the paper cases, but only fill them three-quarters full. Bake for 20–25 minutes, or until a skewer inserted into the centre of a cupcake comes out clean.

Leave to cool in the tin for 5 minutes and then transfer to a wire rack to cool completely before covering with the rosewater glaze.

To make the Rosewater Glaze: Cream together half the icing sugar and all the butter until the mixture resembles fine crumbs, then mix in the milk and rosewater. Finally beat in the remaining icing sugar. Spread the glaze on top of the cupcakes to finish.

PISTACHIO & PRALINE CUPCAKES

These little marvels are so moreish, with a pistachio sponge topped with Italian meringue and nutty praline. They also look very pretty, with the praline shining like jewels.

MAKES 12 CUPCAKES

125g (4fl oz) unsalted butter, softened
175g (6oz) caster sugar
seeds from ½ vanilla pod
75g (3oz) pistachio paste
2 eggs
185g (6½oz) plain flour
1 tsp baking powder
125ml (4fl oz) milk

For the pistachio praline
sunflower oil, for brushing
75g (3oz) unsalted pistachio nuts
200g (7oz) caster sugar
125ml (4fl oz) water

For the meringue topping
150g (5oz) caster sugar
3 tbsp water
generous pinch of cream of tartar
2 egg whites
pinch of salt

Preheat the oven to 200°C/fan 180°C/gas mark 6, and line a cupcake tin with paper cases.

Beat together the butter, sugar, vanilla seeds and pistachio paste until light and creamy. Gradually add the eggs and beat again. Sift in the flour and baking powder, and beat until combined. Add the milk and mix in. Divide the mixture between the paper cases. Bake for 15–17 minutes, or until a skewer inserted into the centre of a cupcake comes out clean. Remove from the tin and transfer to a wire rack to cool.

To make the Pistachio Praline: Line a baking sheet with foil, brush it with sunflower oil and scatter the nuts on top. Place the sugar and water in a saucepan over a low heat, stirring until the sugar has dissolved. Increase the heat and bring to the boil, brushing any sugar crystals down the inside of the pan with a wet pastry brush. Cook for 8–10 minutes or until dark golden. Remove from the heat and pour over the nuts. Leave to cool, then chop into small chunks.

To make the Meringue Topping: Combine the sugar, water and cream of tartar in a heavy-based saucepan, and stir over a medium heat until it boils. Using a sugar thermometer, when the syrup reaches 110°C (230°F), whisk the egg whites, ideally in a free-standing mixer, until stiff. When the syrup reaches 120°C (250°F), with the mixer still on, slowly pour the syrup into the egg whites down the side of the bowl avoiding the whisk. Beat until the meringue is thick, glossy and completely cold, about 10–15 minutes. To decorate, pipe the meringue over the cupcakes (see page 94 for styling tips). Arrange a few nuggets of pistachio praline on top.

CARROT CAKE CUPCAKES

This all-American classic is such a versatile recipe: usually made as a loaf, a round, or baked in a tin as a tray-bake – but now as cupcakes! In a lot of their recipes, our US cousins use oil as a fat which gives you a very moist cake. The cream cheese frosting is rich and delicious, but do make sure you use a very dry cream cheese to give you a nice firm texture. These cakes will keep very well in a tin, but do not store them in the fridge, as they will go hard.

MAKES 12 CUPCAKES

250ml (8fl oz) sunflower or corn oil
225g (7½oz) golden caster sugar
3 eggs
225g (7½oz) self-raising flour
1 tsp ground cinnamon
1 tsp ground nutmeg
250g (8oz) carrots, coarsely grated
100g (3½oz) sultanas, plus extra to decorate
100g (3½oz) chopped walnuts, plus extra to decorate

For the cream cheese frosting
200g (7oz) half-fat cream cheese
100g (3½oz) unrefined golden icing sugar, sifted
finely grated zest of 1 orange

Preheat the oven to 200°C/fan 180°C/gas mark 6, and line a cupcake tin with paper cases.

Pour the oil into a large bowl, add the caster sugar and mix with a large whisk for a few minutes, then add the eggs one at a time.

Sift the flour, cinnamon and nutmeg, and using a large metal spoon, fold the flour into the egg mix. Fold the carrots, sultanas and walnuts into the mixture.

Divide the mixture between the paper cases and bake for 20 minutes, or until a skewer inserted into the centre of a cupcake comes out clean. Leave to cool in the tin for 5 minutes and then transfer to a wire rack to cool completely.

To make the Cream Cheese Frosting: Gently mix the cream cheese until soft and smooth, and then gradually add the icing sugar, followed by the orange zest.

When the cakes are cold, use a small palette knife to spread the frosting on the top of each cake and decorate with few sultanas and walnuts.

CHOCOLATE PEANUT BUTTER CUPCAKES

These cupcakes are just so delicious; the combination of the rich chocolate and the salty crunchy peanut butter work wonderfully.

MAKES 12 CUPCAKES

175g (6oz) unsalted butter
150g (5oz) caster sugar
150g (5oz) light brown sugar
2 eggs
2 tsp vanilla extract
240ml (7¾fl oz) buttermilk
125ml (4fl oz) soured cream
2 tbsp espresso coffee
2 tbsp crunchy peanut butter
250g (8oz) plain flour
100g (3½oz) cocoa powder
1½ tsp baking powder

For the peanut butter frosting
150g (5oz) icing sugar
110g (3¾oz) smooth peanut butter
50g (2oz) unsalted butter,
  softened
¾ tsp vanilla extract
2 tbsp double cream
chopped salted peanuts, to
  decorate

Preheat the oven to 200°C/fan 180°C/gas mark 6, and line a cupcake tin with paper cases.

Cream the butter with both sugars, ideally in the bowl of a free-standing mixer or using an electric hand whisk, on high speed until light and fluffy – about 5 minutes. Lower the speed to medium, and add the eggs one at a time. Then add the vanilla extract and mix in well.

In another bowl, whisk together the buttermilk, soured cream, coffee and peanut butter.

Into a third bowl, sift together the flour, cocoa and baking powder.

On low speed add one-third of the buttermilk mixture followed by one-third of the flour, mix only until just blended. Repeat until all the buttermilk and flour are incorporated. Fold the batter with a spatula to be sure it is completely blended. Divide the batter between the cupcake cases. Bake for 20–25 minutes, or until a skewer inserted into the centre of a cupcake comes out clean. Leave to cool in the tin for 5 minutes, then transfer to a wire rack to cool completely.

To make the Peanut Butter Frosting: Mix the icing sugar, peanut butter, butter and vanilla extract in a free-standing mixer on a medium-low speed until creamy, scraping down the bowl with a spatula as you work – alternatively use an electric hand whisk. Add the cream and beat on high speed until the mixture is light and smooth. Using a piping bag with a small round nozzle, pipe the frosting onto each cupcake (see page 94 for styling tips) and finish with a sprinkling of chopped salted peanuts.

FRUITY
CUPCAKES

KEY LIME CUPCAKES

These fresh, zesty cupcakes make great summer treats. You could add some chopped fresh mint to turn them into Mojito cupcakes, and a cup of roasted coconut in the mix works very well, too. Its a good idea to make the crystallized lime peel decoration the day before you want to serve these cakes.

MAKES 12 CUPCAKES

175g (6oz) unsalted butter, softened
300g (10oz) caster sugar
3 eggs
finely grated zest of 1 lime and 4 tbsp juice
1 tsp vanilla extract
300g (10oz) plain flour
1 tsp baking powder
360ml (12½fl oz) buttermilk

For the crystallized lime peel
2 unwaxed limes
100g (3½oz) caster sugar, plus extra to coat
100ml (3½fl oz) water
For the lime syrup
30g (1¼oz) icing sugar dissolved in the juice of 1½ limes

For the white chocolate frosting
200g (7oz) white chocolate, broken into pieces
125ml (4fl oz) whipping cream
175g (6oz) unsalted butter, softened
grated zest of 1 lime and juice of ½
350g (11½oz) icing sugar

First make the Crystallized Lime Peel: Pare the peel from each lime, then carefully cut it into thin strips. Put the caster sugar and the water in a pan and bring to the boil, stirring. Once bubbling, add one-third of the lime peel and cook for 3–4 minutes. Remove the peel, roll gently in caster sugar and lay them on greaseproof paper. (Don't arrange them on top of each other or they will stick together.) Repeat with the remaining peel and leave to dry overnight.

Preheat the oven to 200°C/fan 180°C/gas mark 6, and line a cupcake tin with paper cases.

Using a free-standing mixer or electric hand whisk, cream the butter and sugar until pale and fluffy. Add the eggs, slowly, one at the time. Then add the lime zest and juice, and the vanilla extract. In another bowl, sift together the flour and baking powder. Gradually add this to the butter mixture with alternate spoonfuls of buttermilk. Divide the mixture between the paper cases and bake for 25–30 minutes, or until a skewer inserted into the centre of a cupcake comes out clean. Leave to cool in the tins for 5 minutes then transfer to a wire rack. Whilst warm, use a cocktail stick to insert small holes all over each cupcake, spoon over a teaspoon of lime syrup and allow it to soak and cool before frosting.

To make the frosting: Melt the chocolate with the cream in a heatproof bowl over a saucepan of simmering water, making sure the bowl does not touch the surface of the water. Allow to cool completely. Then whisk in the butter, lime zest, juice and icing sugar. When smooth, use a piping bag to pipe the frosting onto each cake, and decorate with a few strands of crystallized lime peel.

ZESTY LEMON & WHITE CHOCOLATE CUPCAKES

This light and zesty sponge carries off the rich white chocolate frosting with serious style, making a great summer dessert.

MAKES 12 CUPCAKES

160g (5½oz) unsalted butter, softened
100g (3½oz) caster sugar
2 eggs
200ml (7fl oz) natural yoghurt
grated zest of 1 lemon and 2 tsp lemon juice
½ tsp lemon oil
200g (7oz) plain flour
1 tsp baking powder
2 tsp poppy seeds
½ a 320g jar of lemon curd

For the white chocolate frosting
75g (3oz) unsalted butter
75g (3oz) cream cheese
150g (5oz) icing sugar
100g (3½oz) white chocolate, melted, plus extra to decorate

Preheat the oven to 200°C/fan 180°C/gas mark 6, and line a cupcake tin with paper cases.

In a large bowl, cream the butter and sugar together until light and fluffy. Then mix in the eggs, one at a time, followed by the yoghurt, lemon zest and juice and the lemon oil. Sift the flour and baking powder together and stir this into the butter mixture with the poppy seeds until just combined.

Divide the mixture between the paper cases, just filling them half-full. Spoon some lemon curd over each and then top to the rim with the remaining batter. Bake for about 25–30 minutes, or until a skewer inserted into the side of a cupcake comes out clean. Leave to cool in the tins for 5 minutes then transfer to a wire rack and allow to cool completely before frosting.

To make the White Chocolate Frosting: Cream together the butter, cream cheese and icing sugar, then add the melted white chocolate. Either spread the frosting using a small palette knife or pipe the frosting over the cooled cupcakes. Sprinkle with white chocolate curls and leave to set.

ORANGE MARMALADE CUPCAKES

This could almost be a breakfast cupcake! When I can get hold of it I make mine with blood orange marmalade and a homemade version make these cupcakes even more divine.

MAKES 12 CUPCAKES

150g (5oz) unsalted butter,
  softened
100g (3½oz) golden caster sugar
2 eggs
finely grated zest of 2 oranges
  and 2 tbsp juice
3 tbsp Seville orange marmalade,
  plus extra to decorate
1 tsp vanilla extract
250g (8oz) self-raising flour

For the frosting
1 quantity Vanilla Buttercream
  Frosting (see page 84)
finely grated zest of 1 orange

Preheat the oven to 200°C/fan 180°C/gas mark 6, and line a cupcake tin with paper cases.

In a large bowl, cream together the butter and sugar. Add the eggs one at a time. Mix in the orange zest and juice, the marmalade and vanilla extract. Sift the flour into the mixture and combine until smooth.

Divide the mixture between the paper cupcake cases and bake for about 20–25 minutes, until a skewer inserted into the centre of a cupcake comes out clean. Leave to cool in the tin for 5 minutes and then transfer to a wire rack and allow to cool completely before frosting.

Decorate the cupcakes with Vanilla Buttercream Frosting mixed with the orange zest, and top each cupcake with a teaspoon of marmalade.

ORANGE & PUMPKIN CUPCAKES

Perfect for Hallowe'en celebrations, this is a nice autumn recipe. You can find tins of cooked pumpkin in specialist food stores, especially those that have American foods sections.

MAKES 12 CUPCAKES

300g (10oz) plain flour
1 tbsp baking powder
½ tsp bicarbonate of soda
½ tsp ground ginger
¾ tsp ground cinnamon
½ tsp ground nutmeg
grated zest of 1 orange
100g (3½oz) unsalted butter, softened
200g (7oz) caster sugar
2 eggs
225g (7½oz) cooked and mashed or canned pumpkin
175ml (6fl oz) milk

For the mascarpone frosting
300g (10oz) mascarpone cheese
75g (3oz) icing sugar, sifted
grated zest of 1 orange and
   1 tbsp juice

Preheat the oven to 200°C/fan 180°C/gas mark 6, and line a cupcake tin with paper cases.

In a large bowl, sift together the flour, baking powder, bicarbonate of soda, ginger, cinnamon and nutmeg, then stir in the grated orange zest.

In another bowl, cream together the butter and sugar until light and fluffy. Then beat in the eggs, one at a time. Blend the pumpkin into this mixture and then stir in the sifted dry ingredients, a little at a time, alternating with some of the milk, blending after each addition, until the batter is smooth.

Divide the mixture between the paper cases and bake for 25 minutes, or until a skewer inserted into the centre of a cupcake comes out clean. Leave to cool in the tin for 5 minutes then transfer to a wire rack and allow to cool completely before frosting.

To make the Mascarpone Frosting: Beat the mascarpone cheese until light and smooth, and then gradually add the icing sugar, stirring after each addition. Stir in the grated orange zest and juice, and mix until smooth. Using a small palette knife, spread the frosting over each cake.

LEMON MERINGUE CUPCAKES

The classic lemon meringue pie turned into a delicious cupcake... why not serve these as a dessert and add a few berries for an extra finishing touch.

MAKES 12 CUPCAKES

100g (3½oz) unsalted butter, softened
100g (3½oz) caster sugar
seeds from 1 vanilla pod
2 eggs
100g (3½oz) self-raising flour, sifted
finely grated zest of 1 lemon, plus a few strips to decorate
75g (3oz) lemon curd

For the meringue
2 egg whites
100g (3½oz) caster sugar

Preheat the oven to 200°C/fan 180°C/gas mark 6, and line a cupcake tin with paper cases.

In a large mixing bowl, ideally using an electric hand whisk, cream together the butter, sugar and vanilla seeds until the mixture is pale, fluffy and well combined. Crack in the eggs one at a time, and beat in until both are fully incorporated into the mixture. Fold in the sifted flour and the lemon zest until well combined.

Divide the mixture between the paper cases and add a teaspoonful of lemon curd to the top of each cupcake. Bake for 15–20 minutes, or until they are pale golden-brown and spring back when pressed lightly in the centre.

While the cupcakes are baking, make the meringue: Whisk the egg whites until they form soft peaks. Gradually add the sugar, whisking continuously, until stiff peaks form again. The mixture should be thick and glossy.

When the cakes have cooked, turn off the oven and preheat the grill to its highest setting.

Spoon the meringue into a piping bag with a small plain nozzle and pipe it on top of each cupcake. To create a spikey effect, pipe small dots in a circle around the rim, pushing the bag down and up sharply to make a point, then repeat in a spiral until you reach the centre.

Place the cupcakes under a hot grill for 2 minutes to colour the meringue (or you can use a kitchen blow-torch).

STRAWBERRY & CREAM CUPCAKES

The great British tradition of strawberries and cream in a cheeky cupcake. These are perfect for an al fresco lunch or picnic.

MAKES 12 CUPCAKES

175g (6oz) unsalted butter, softened
175g (6oz) caster sugar
3 eggs, beaten
1 tsp vanilla extract
175g (6oz) self-raising flour, sifted

For the frosting
175g (6oz) strawberries, plus 6 extra to decorate
300g (10oz) full-fat cream cheese
225g (7½oz) icing sugar, sifted

Preheat the oven to 200°C/fan 180°C/gas mark 6, and line a cupcake tin with paper cases.

Cream the butter and sugar together until light and fluffy, then gradually beat in the eggs. When the eggs have been incorporated add the vanilla extract and fold in the flour.

Divide the mixture between the paper cases and bake for about 20 minutes, or until they have risen and are golden. Leave to cool in the tins for 5 minutes then transfer to a wire rack and allow to cool completely before frosting.

To make the frosting: Blend or mash the strawberries to a purée, then pass through a fine-meshed sieve to remove the seeds. Beat the cream cheese, icing sugar and strawberry purée together to form a smooth and shiny icing. Transfer to a piping bag and pipe the frosting on to the cooled cakes (see page 94 for piping tips), then top each cupcake with half a strawberry.

BLUEBERRY COMPOTE CUPCAKES

I like to add the berries in the centre of these delicious blueberry compote 'kiss cakes', in order to enhance the flavour and provide a nice surprise when biting into the cupcake. I have decorated these with chocolate lips painted with red edible colouring, but you can top yours with whatever you like.

MAKES 12 CUPCAKES

2 eggs
200g (7oz) caster sugar
125ml (4fl oz) sunflower oil
¼ tsp vanilla extract
250g (8oz) plain flour
pinch of salt
½ tsp baking powder
250ml (8fl oz) soured cream
1 quantity Vanilla Buttercream
   Frosting (see page 84)

For the blueberry compote
150g (5oz) blueberries
50g (2oz) caster sugar

First make the Blueberry Compote: Place the blueberries and the sugar in a small saucepan over a low heat and cook gently until the fruits start to pop, stirring to prevent the sugar from catching. Leave to cool. If your compote has produced a lot of liquid, strain a little into a bowl so not to add too much extra liquid to your cakes (this spare juice will come in handy later!).

Preheat the oven to 200°C/fan 180°C/gas mark 6, and line a cupcake tin with paper cases.

In a large bowl, beat the eggs, gradually adding the sugar while beating. Continue beating and slowly pour in the oil. Stir in the vanilla extract. In a separate bowl sift together the flour, salt and baking powder. Stir these dry ingredients into the egg mixture in small amounts alternating with the soured cream.

Spoon some of the mixture into the paper cases just to fill them half full, then spoon 1½ teaspoons of the compote on top. Top each with another spoonful of batter to cover and fill almost to the top of the case.

Cook for 25 minutes, or until a skewer inserted into the side of a cupcake comes out clean. Leave to cool in the tins for 5 minutes then transfer to a wire rack and allow to cool completely before frosting.

Pipe Vanilla Buttercream Frosting in spirals on top of each cupcake and spoon over any excess compote you have remaining and some of the lovely blueberry juice.

RHUBARB CUPCAKES

For this recipe you must get the beautiful stalks of red/pink 'champagne' rhubarb that are in season at the beginning of the year. As well as being less fibrous, this gives a lovely colour to these cute cupcakes.

MAKES 12 CUPCAKES

250g (8oz) unsalted butter, softened
175g (6oz) soft brown sugar
3 eggs
225g (7½oz) self-raising flour
2 tsp ground ginger
175ml (6fl oz) milk
1 quantity Vanilla Buttercream Frosting (see page 84)

For the baked rhubarb strips
2 stalks of pink rhubarb
icing sugar, for dusting

For the rhubarb compote
125g (4oz) rhubarb, trimmed and cut into small dice
30g (1¼oz) caster sugar
1 tsp ground ginger
1 tbsp water

It is best to make the baked rhubarb strips the day before: Preheat the oven to 120°C/fan 100°C/gas mark ½. With a very sharp knife, cut the rhubarb stalks into 10cm (4-inch) pieces and then cut very thin lengths from each piece. Place on a baking tray lined with baking paper or a silicone mat, dust icing sugar over the top and bake for 2–3 hours, or until dried out and crisp. Be careful not to overcook or you will lose the beautiful pink shade.

Preheat the oven to 200°C/fan 180°C/gas mark 6, and line a cupcake tin with paper cases.

Cream the butter and sugar until pale and fluffy. Add the eggs and then slowly add the milk. Sift in the flour and ginger. Divide the mixture between the paper cases and bake for 18–20 minutes, or until a skewer inserted into the centre of a cupcake comes out clean. Leave to cool in the tin for 5 minutes then transfer to a wire rack and allow to cool completely.

To make the Rhubarb Compote: Place all the ingredients in a small pan and heat gently to boiling point (you just want the rhubarb to release its natural juices and turn a beautiful shade of pink). Leave to bubble and reduce for 2–3 minutes. Once the rhubarb has softened and the liquid has gone syrupy, remove from the heat and leave to cool completely.

Use a 2cm- (¾ inch-) wide cutter to cut 1cm (⅓ inch) deep into the centre of each cupcake to leave a space for the compote. Spoon the compote into these spaces and then pipe vanilla frosting over the top. Once the frosting has set, arrange the dried pieces of baked rhubarb decoratively on top of each cupcake.

APPLE CRUMBLE CUPCAKES

With their crumbly topping, these are more of a dessert than a cupcake – you could even serve them hot with runny custard.

MAKES 12 CUPCAKES

2 cooking apples, peeled, cored and chopped
1 tsp ground cinnamon
½ tsp bicarbonate of soda
100g (3½oz) butter, softened
200g (7oz) soft brown sugar
2 eggs
350g (11½oz) self-raising flour
icing sugar, for dusting

For the crumble topping
50g (2oz) plain flour
50g (2oz) soft brown sugar
½ tsp ground cinnamon
40g (1½oz) cold unsalted butter

Preheat the oven to 200°C/fan 180°C/gas mark 6, and line a cupcake tin with paper cases.

First make the crumble topping; put the flour, sugar and cinnamon in a bowl. With your fingertips, rub the unsalted butter into the flour mix until the mixture resembles breadcrumbs. Set this mixture to one side.

Put the apples in a saucepan with the cinnamon and cook over a gentle heat until mushy. Leave to cool, then drain through a fine-meshed sieve to remove any liquid, then weigh out 250g (8oz) of the apple.

In a bowl, mix the bicarbonate of soda into the apples. In a large bowl, cream the butter and sugar together, and then add the eggs. Fold the self-raising flour and the apples alternately into the butter mixture and mix well.

Divide the mixture between the paper cases. Sprinkle the crumble mix over the tops and bake for 20–25 minutes, or until golden brown on top and a skewer inserted into the centre of a cupcake comes out clean.

Leave to cool in the tins for 5 minutes then transfer to a wire rack and allow to cool completely. When cool, finish with a dusting of icing sugar.

MAURITIUS PINEAPPLE CUPCAKES

This recipe is inspired by a fabulous dessert of spit-roasted baby pineapple with Amaretto that I once had in Mauritius... all the flavours are here in these cupcakes.

MAKES 12 CUPCAKES

175g (6oz) plain flour
30g (1¼oz) ground almonds
1 tsp baking powder
125g (4oz) unsalted butter, softened
300g (10oz) golden caster sugar
3 eggs at room temperature
1 tsp pure vanilla extract
½ tsp pure almond extract
125ml (4fl oz) milk
90ml (3fl oz) Amaretto
400ml (14fl oz) double cream

For the flambéed pineapple
100g (3½oz) caster sugar
1 small pineapple, peeled, cored and cut into small dice
100ml (3½fl oz) Amaretto
100ml (3½fl oz) double cream
1 tbsp fresh orange juice
seeds from 1 vanilla pod

Preheat the oven to 200°C/fan 180°C/gas mark 6, and line a cupcake tin with paper cases.

In a bowl, mix together the flour, ground almonds and baking powder. In another large bowl, cream the butter and sugar until pale and fluffy. Add the eggs, one at a time, beating until each is incorporated. Mix in the vanilla and almond extracts. Add the flour mixture in three batches, alternating with the milk in two additions, and mixing until just combined. If using an electric hand whisk, reduce the speed to low.

Divide the mixture between the paper cases, to fill each three-quarters full. Bake for 18–20 minutes, or until a skewer inserted into the centre of a cupcake comes out clean. Set the tin on a wire rack and immediately poke little holes over the tops of the cupcakes with a cocktail stick then pour a teaspoon of Amaretto over the tops. Allow to cool completely before removing from the tin.

To make the Flambéed Pineapple: In a large pan, heat the sugar over a medium heat, stirring, until the sugar dissolves and turns golden brown. Add the chopped pineapple and carefully toss it in the dissolved sugar. Carefully pour in the Amaretto and ignite the alcohol. Once the flames subside and the caramel melts, if there is a lot of liquid in the pan at this stage strain a little away. Then stir in the cream, orange juice and vanilla seeds. Boil, stirring occasionally, until thickened, for about 5 minutes. Remove from the heat and allow to cool completely. When ready to serve, whip the cream to soft peaks and spread over the top of each cooled cupcake. Top with a generous spoonful of Flambéed Pineapple.

RICH & SPICY
CUPCAKES

MEXICAN CHOCOLATE CUPCAKES

The rich chocolate and all the lovely exotic spices in these cakes work very well together, and just when you thought you'd tasted everything, a lovely hot sensation hits you as the cayenne chilli-flavoured frosting works its wonders... another one for adults only!

MAKES 12 CUPCAKES

175g (6oz) plain flour
225g (7½oz) caster sugar
4 tbsp cocoa powder
1 tsp bicarbonate of soda
1 tsp cinnamon
¼ tsp ground nutmeg
1 tsp vanilla extract
1 tbsp white wine vinegar
5 tbsp sunflower oil
chilli pepper cake decorations,
  to decorate

For the frosting
100g (3½oz) dark chocolate,
  broken into pieces
150g (5oz) unsalted butter
150g (5oz) icing sugar
¼ tsp ground cayenne pepper

Preheat the oven to 200°C/fan 180°C/gas mark 6, and line a cupcake tin with paper cases.

Sift together the flour, sugar, cocoa, bicarbonate of soda, cinnamon and nutmeg into a bowl. In a large bowl, blend together the vanilla extract, vinegar, oil and 250ml (8fl oz) cold water. Mix the dry ingredients into this mixture until well combined and the batter is smooth – a free-standing mixer or an electric hand whisk will help in doing this.

Divide the mixture between the paper cases (it will be fairly liquid, so you may want to use a jug) and bake for 20–25 minutes, or until a skewer inserted into the centre of a cupcake comes out clean. Allow to cool in the tin for 5 minutes, and then transfer to a wire rack to cool completely.

To make the frosting: Melt the chocolate in a heatproof bowl placed over a saucepan of barely simmering water, making sure the bowl does not touch the surface of the water. When melted leave to cool.

Whisk the butter and icing sugar together until pale and fluffy, then whisk in the cooled melted chocolate and the cayenne pepper. Pipe the frosting onto the cooled cakes and top with chilli pepper cake decorations to finish.

TIRAMISU CUPCAKES

This is my favourite Italian dessert in a cupcake. The light coffee sponge topped with a mascarpone and Marsala frosting makes a quite delicious combination. These cupcakes must be eaten on the day they are made.

MAKES 12 CUPCAKES

50g (2oz) unsalted butter
125g (4oz) golden caster sugar
4 eggs
125g (4oz) plain flour
1 level tbsp instant espresso
   granules dissolved in 2 tsp
   boiling water
cocoa powder, to decorate
icing sugar, to decorate

For the frosting
250g (8oz) mascarpone
125g (4oz) golden icing sugar,
   sifted
1 tbsp Marsala wine

Preheat the oven to 200°C/fan 180°C/gas mark 6, and line a cupcake tin with paper cases.

Put the butter in a heatproof bowl and melt in the microwave or in a heatproof bowl placed over a saucepan of barely simmering water, making sure the bowl does not touch the surface of the water.

Put the sugar and eggs in another bowl and, ideally using a free-standing mixer or an electric hand whisk, cream them together until light and frothy and doubled in volume – this will take several minutes.

Sift the flour and gently fold half of it into the mixture. Mix the coffee into the melted butter and pour half of this into the mixture. Add the remaining flour, followed by the rest of the coffee and butter mix. Gently fold these in.

Divide the mixture between the paper cases and bake for 25 minutes, or until a skewer inserted into the centre of a cupcake comes out clean. Leave to cool in the tin for 5 minutes and then turn the cupcakes out on a wire rack and allow to cool completely.

To make the frosting: Whisk the mascarpone with the golden icing sugar, then add the Marsala and mix until combined. Spread this on top of each cupcake and finish with a generous dusting of cocoa powder and icing sugar on top.

MOCHA CUPCAKES

Dark chocolate and coffee always make a good combination, so I've put these two fabulous flavours together to create the most delicious cupcakes.

MAKES 12 CUPCAKES

175g (6oz) unsalted butter,
  softened
175g (6oz) caster sugar
3 eggs
1 tbsp hot water mixed with
  1 tsp instant coffee
150g (5oz) plain flour
25g (1oz) cocoa powder

For the frosting
100g (3½oz) unsalted butter,
  softened
150g (5oz) icing sugar
2 tsp fresh coffee, ideally
  espresso, cooled
50g (2oz) melted dark chocolate
chocolate coffee beans,
  to decorate
edible gold paint, to decorate
  (optional, see page 127 for
  stockists)

Preheat the oven to 200°C/fan 180°C/gas mark 6, and line a cupcake tin with paper cases.

Cream the butter and sugar together until light and fluffy, then add the eggs one at the time, beating well after each addition until combined and the mixture is smooth. Stir in the coffee mixture. Sift the flour and cocoa powder over the mixture and fold in.

Divide the mixture between the paper cases and bake for 20 minutes, or until a skewer inserted into the centre of a cupcake comes out clean. Leave to cool in the tin for 5 minutes and then turn the cupcakes out on a wire rack and allow to cool completely.

To make the frosting: Beat the butter and icing sugar together until pale and fluffy. Add the coffee and melted chocolate, and beat until smooth. Pipe or spoon this on the top of each cupcake and finish by decorating with some chocolate coffee beans that have been lightly painted with edible gold paint.

STEM GINGER CUPCAKES

This powerful recipe will give any afternoon tea or party a punchy start! The addition of the preserved stem ginger makes this little wonder very moist and moreish.

MAKES 18 CUPCAKES

250g (8oz) unsalted butter
250g (8oz) dark brown soft sugar
250g (8oz) black treacle
300ml (½ pint) milk
3 eggs, lightly beaten
100g (3½oz) preserved stem ginger, drained and finely chopped, plus extra to decorate
400g (13oz) plain flour
2 tsp baking powder
1 tsp mixed spice
2 tsp ground ginger
1½ quantities Vanilla Buttercream Frosting (see page 84)

Preheat the oven to 200°C/fan 180°C/gas mark 6, and line a 12-hole and a 6-hole cupcake tin with paper cases.

Put the butter, sugar and treacle in a saucepan and heat gently for about 5 minutes until the butter and sugar have melted. Stir in the milk and leave to cool before beating in the eggs.

Mix the chopped ginger and remaining ingredients together in a large bowl. Pour in the melted mixture and, using a wooden spoon, mix together to form a smooth thick batter.

Divide the mixture between the paper cases and bake for about 25 minutes, or until a skewer inserted into the centre of a cupcake comes out clean. Leave to cool in the tins for 5 minutes then transfer to a wire rack and allow to cool completely before frosting.

I like to finish mine with Vanilla Buttercream Frosting, and with some more finely chopped stem ginger sprinkled on the top.

LADY GREY CUPCAKES

This light and fruity cupcake has just the right balance of the tea flavour. The delicate Italian glacé fruits have been soaked in orange liqueur and look like jewels on top, adding a splash of glamour.

MAKES 12 CUPCAKES

150g (5oz) mixed glacé fruit, finely chopped, plus extra to decorate
2–3 tbsp orange liqueur
200ml (7fl oz) water
2 Lady Grey tea bags
2 eggs
200g (7oz) golden caster sugar
125ml (4fl oz) vegetable oil
1 tsp vanilla extract
250g (8oz) plain flour
½ tsp baking powder

For the topping
1 quantity Cream Cheese Frosting (see page 85)
edible gold leaf (see page 127 for stockists)

The day before you want to bake, in a small bowl, mix together the chopped glacé fruits and the orange liqueur, and leave to soak overnight.

Bring the water to the boil and pour it over the tea bags in a small bowl. Leave to infuse to create a strong tea. Allow to cool.

Preheat the oven to 200°C/fan 180°C/gas mark 6, and line a cupcake tin with paper cases.

In a large bowl, beat the eggs and gradually add the sugar while still beating. Continue beating while slowly pouring in the oil. Stir in the vanilla extract. Sift the flour and baking powder together. Fold these into the mixture a little at a time, alternating with additions of some of the strong tea, until the mixture is nice and smooth.

Drain the glacé fruits, reserving the orange liqueur. Fold the fruits into the cake mixture and divide the mixture between the paper cases. Bake for 20 minutes, or until a skewer inserted into a cupcake comes out clean. Once the cupcakes have cooked and whilst still warm, pierce their tops several times with a cocktail stick and spoon over the reserved orange liqueur. Leave to cool in the tin before decorating.

Pipe Cream Cheese Frosting on top of each cupcake and decorate with flecks of edible gold leaf to finish.

LIQUORICE CUPCAKES

If you enjoy the rich flavour of liquorice, this recipe is for you. I like using these cupcakes as my base for Hallowe'en cakes because of the natural dark colour of the sponge and icing.

MAKES 16 CUPCAKES

100g (3½oz) pure liquorice
   sweets
185ml (6½fl oz) milk
250g (8oz) unsalted butter,
   softened
50g (2oz) dark muscovado sugar
4 eggs
185g (7½oz) self-raising flour
60g (2½oz) plain flour

For the liquorice frosting
100g (3½oz) pure liquorice
   sweets, plus some strands
   to decorate
50g (2oz) icing sugar
50g (2oz) unsalted butter,
   softened

Preheat the oven to 200°C/fan 180°C/gas mark 6, and line a 12-hole and a 4-hole cupcake tin with paper cases.

Place the liquorice sweets and the milk in a saucepan and heat gently, stirring, until the sweets have dissolved. Leave to cool.

Place the butter and sugar in a bowl and cream together until pale and creamy. Add the eggs one at a time, beating well after each addition until well combined and the mixture is smooth. Sift the flours together and fold into the mixture together with the cool liquorice milk. Stir until smooth.

Divide the mixture between the paper cases to fill them three-quarters full and bake for 20 minutes, or until a skewer inserted into the centre of a cupcake comes out clean. Leave to cool in the tins for 5 minutes then transfer to a wire rack and allow to cool completely before frosting.

To make the Liquorice Frosting: Place the liquorice sweets in a heatproof bowl and place over a saucepan of barely simmering water, making sure the bowl does not touch the surface of the water. Heat until completely dissolved, stirring occasionally. Remove from the heat and allow to cool.

Using a whisk, whip the icing sugar and butter together until pale and smooth. Still mixing, add in the dissolved liquorice and beat until smooth.

Pipe or spoon the frosting on top of the cooled cupcakes and decorate with strands of liquorice.

MADAGASCAN VANILLA CUPCAKES

This is a classic cupcake that could be a safe base for any topping – and we all have a day when a good simple vanilla cupcake does the trick!

MAKES 12 CUPCAKES

250g (8oz) unsalted butter, softened
250g (8oz) caster sugar
4 eggs
1 tsp vanilla extract, preferably Madagascan
185g (6½oz) self-raising flour
60g (2½oz) plain flour
185ml (6½fl oz) milk
1 quantity Vanilla Buttercream Frosting (see page 84) or Cream Cheese Frosting (see page 85)
sugar cake decorations, to decorate

Preheat the oven to 200°C/fan 180°C/gas mark 6, and line a cupcake tin with paper cases.

Place the butter and sugar in a bowl and cream together until pale and creamy. Add the eggs, one at a time, then add the vanilla extract and beat until well combined. Sift in the flours together and fold in, a little at a time, alternating with some of the milk. Stir until smooth.

Divide the mixture between the paper cases and bake for 20 minutes, or until a skewer inserted into the centre of a cupcake comes out clean. Leave to cool in the tin for 5 minutes, then transfer to a wire rack and allow to cool completely before frosting.

Pipe Vanilla Buttercream Frosting or Cream Cheese Frosting on top, and sprinkle over sugar decorations to finish.

SALTED CARAMEL CUPCAKES

One of the most popular flavours in Brittany, where I come from, is salted butter caramel. I grew up eating ice cream, sweets and spreads flavoured by this now very fashionable combination. These cupcakes are so decadent with a rich caramel sauce poured over the top.

MAKES 12 CUPCAKES

175g (6oz) self-raising flour
1 tsp bicarbonate of soda
75g (3oz) unsalted butter, softened
100g (3½oz) muscovado sugar
2 eggs, lightly beaten
1 tsp vanilla extract
2 tbsp milk
50g (2oz) toffee or fudge pieces, chopped small

For the caramel sauce
125g (4oz) caster sugar
75g (3oz) salted butter
5 tbsp double cream
1 tsp vanilla extract

For the buttercream frosting
150g (5oz) unsalted butter, softened
150g (5oz) icing sugar
1 tsp vanilla extract
1 tsp caramel extract (optional)
few flakes of sea salt, to decorate

Preheat the oven to 200°C/fan 180°C/gas mark 6, and line a cupcake tin with paper cases.

Sift the flour and bicarbonate of soda together into a bowl and set aside. Using a free-standing mixer or an electric hand whisk, cream together the butter and sugar together for a good 5 minutes until very light and fluffy. Add the beaten eggs gradually, beating between each addition and adding 1 tablespoon of flour about halfway through to prevent curdling. Beat in the vanilla extract. Lastly fold in the remaining flour, the milk and the toffee/fudge pieces.

Divide the mixture between the paper cases and bake for 15–20 minutes, or until the tops spring back when pressed with a finger. Leave to cool in the tin for 5 minutes, then transfer to a wire rack and allow to cool completely.

To make the Caramel Sauce: Dissolve the sugar in 4 tablespoons of water in a small heavy-based saucepan over a gentle heat. Increase the heat and simmer until you have a nice blonde caramel. Immediately remove from the heat. Add the butter, taking care as it may splutter. Keep stirring as you add the cream and vanilla extract, until smooth. Leave to cool.

To make the Buttercream Frosting: Cream the butter and icing sugar together for at least 5 minutes and beat in the vanilla and caramel extracts.

Use a small palette knife to spread Buttercream Frosting on top of the cupcakes. Pour a little Caramel Sauce over the top, and sprinkle with a few sea salt flakes to finish.

FUSION CUPCAKES

Since travelling more often to the Far East, I have really begun to enjoy the taste of Asian food. The fusion of sweet and sour flavours works so well in traditional Asian cooking, and in these delicious cupcakes, too.

MAKES 12 CUPCAKES

5cm (2 inch) piece of fresh root
  ginger, peeled
2 lemon grass stalks, trimmed
  and roughly chopped
2 tsp vanilla extract
100g (3½oz) butter, softened
175g (6oz) golden caster sugar
2 eggs
200g (7oz) self-raising flour
125ml (4fl oz) milk

For the frosting
100g (3½oz) butter, softened
350g (11½oz) icing sugar
3 tbsp milk
1 tsp vanilla extract
100g (3½oz) mixed exotic dried
  fruits (such as mango, coconut
  or pineapple), to decorate

Preheat the oven to 200°C/fan 180°C/gas mark 6, and line a cupcake tin with paper cases.

Place the ginger, lemon grass and vanilla extract in a food processor and process until you get a fine paste. Push through a sieve to extract the juice and discard the pulp.

Cream the butter and sugar together until light and fluffy. Add the reserved juice, then add the eggs one at a time, beating slowly until just combined. Add the flour and milk in alternate batches and stir with a wooden spoon until just combined.

Divide the mixture between the paper cases and bake for 15–20 minutes, or until a skewer inserted into the centre of a cupcake comes out clean. Leave to cool in the tin for 5 minutes, then transfer to a wire rack and allow to cool completely before frosting.

To make the frosting: Beat the butter until very pale, then gradually beat in the icing sugar. Add the milk and vanilla extract and beat until well combined.

Use a small palette knife or piping bag to decorate the cakes with the frosting. Roughly chop the dried fruit and arrange on top.

STICKY TOFFEE CUPCAKES

One of my favourite things about the arrival of gastropubs is the rebirth of proper English 'puds'. When properly made, they are rich, filling and so indulgent. This one is my winter perfection and, because the cakes are cute and tiny, you won't feel guilty about eating them. These actually need to be made in smaller standard cupcake cases and not the larger 'muffin' type.

MAKES 12 STANDARD CUPCAKES

150ml (¼ pint) hot water
1 tea bag
50g (2oz) dried apricots, roughly chopped
50g (2oz) dates, stoned and roughly chopped
150g (5oz) self-raising flour
1 tsp baking powder
50g (2oz) muscovado sugar
1 tbsp golden syrup
2 large eggs, lightly beaten
50g (2oz) butter, melted

For the toffee sauce
50g (2oz) caster sugar
50g (2oz) butter
100ml (3½fl oz) double cream
pouring cream, to serve

Preheat the oven to 200°C/fan 180°C/gas mark 6, and line a standard bun tin with paper cases.

Put the hot water, tea bag, apricots and dates in a saucepan, bring to the boil, then remove from the heat and leave to soak and cool.

Sift the flour and baking powder together into a large mixing bowl. Drain the fruits, then add them to the flour with the muscovado sugar, golden syrup, eggs and butter, then mix together until blended.

Divide the mixture between the paper cases and bake for 25–30 minutes, or until a skewer inserted into the centre of a cupcake comes out clean.

Towards the end of the cupcake cooking time, make the toffee sauce: heat the caster sugar in a heavy-based saucepan until you get a dark caramel. Add the butter, stirring well with a wooden spoon. Deglaze the pan by stirring in the double cream. When all the caramel has dissolved, pass the sauce through a sieve into a warm serving jug.

When the cupcakes are cooked, carefully remove the paper cases and serve immediately, piping hot, with the toffee sauce and lots of pouring cream.

GUILT-FREE
CUPCAKES

ANGEL FOOD CUPCAKES WITH RASPBERRY FROSTING

This fat-free sponge recipe is very light and delicate... like an angel! The raspberry frosting adds a great fruity touch to these cupcakes, making them perfect for summer.

MAKES 12 CUPCAKES

115g (3½oz) plain flour
85g (3¼oz) icing sugar
1 tsp cream of tartar
8 egg whites
pinch of salt
150g (5oz) caster sugar
½ tsp vanilla extract
½ tsp almond extract

For the raspberry frosting
100g (3½oz) fresh raspberries, plus extra to decorate
125g (4oz) unsalted butter, softened and diced
225g (7½oz) icing sugar, sifted, plus more to decorate

Preheat the oven to 200°C/fan 180°C/gas mark 6, and line a cupcake tin with paper cases.

Sift the flour, icing sugar and cream of tartar into a bowl and set aside. In a large bowl whisk the egg whites until frothy, ideally using a free-standing mixer or an electric hand whisk. Then add the salt and gradually begin to add the caster sugar a tablespoonful at a time. Continue whisking until stiff peaks form – this will take several minutes.

Stir in the vanilla and almond extracts, then add the flour and icing sugar mixture. Fold the mixture gently with a large metal spoon until combined. It's important to do this quickly – if the mixture is left to stand, it will collapse and spoil the light consistency of the cakes.

Divide the mixture between the paper cases and bake for 15–20 minutes, or until a skewer inserted into the centre of a cupcake comes out clean. Leave to cool in the tin for 5 minutes, then transfer to a wire rack and allow to cool completely. These cakes will sink a little as they cool.

To make the Raspberry Frosting: Rub the raspberries through a fine-meshed sieve to yield about 2 tablespoons of raspberry purée. Add the butter to a clean bowl and cream until soft. Sift some of the icing sugar over the top, then beat in to combine. Repeat this process until all the sugar has been incorporated into the butter. Then beat in the raspberry purée to give a spreading consistency.

Using a piping bag with a plain nozzle, pipe the frosting (see page 94 for piping tips), and decorate with fresh raspberries and a dusting of icing sugar.

LOW-FAT CHOCOLATE CUPCAKES

I think that if I was on a diet, I would miss chocolate the most. But don't worry, you can spoil yourself with this recipe… but not too often!

MAKES 12 CUPCAKES

100g (3½oz) plain flour
25g (1oz) cocoa powder
4 large eggs
125g (4oz) caster sugar
25g (1oz) chocolate chips

For the topping
75g (3oz) low-fat spread
150g (5oz) low-fat cream cheese
100g (3½oz) dark chocolate
  (70% cocoa solids), melted
  and cooled
artificial sweetener, to taste

Preheat the oven to 200°C/fan 180°C/gas mark 6, and line a cupcake tin with paper cases.

Sift together the flour and cocoa powder. In a large bowl, whisk together the eggs and sugar using an electric hand whisk until the mixture becomes thick, foamy and has doubled in size. This may take up to 10 minutes, but it is worth it, as the more air that gets in the lighter the sponge will be. Gently fold in the flour and cocoa powder followed by the chocolate chips, taking care to knock out as little air as possible.

Divide the mixture between the paper cases and bake for 20 minutes, or until a skewer inserted into the centre of a cupcake comes out clean. Leave to cool in the tin for 5 minutes, then transfer to a wire rack and allow to cool completely.

To make the topping: Mix the low-fat spread with the cream cheese, then stir in the cooled melted chocolate. Sweeten to taste with the artificial sweetener, then spread over the top of the cupcakes.

LOW-FAT WHITE CHOCOLATE & BERRY CUPCAKES

As much as I always try not to compromise on ingredients, it is possible to still indulge yourself even if you are following a low-fat diet. Despite being low in fat, these cupcakes are delicious, light and tasty. They won't make you feel guilty and one is much more enjoyable than an apple!

MAKES 12 CUPCAKES

100g (3½oz) low-fat spread
100g (3½oz) golden caster sugar
175g (6oz) self-raising flour, sifted
2 eggs
½ tsp vanilla extract
4 tbsp skimmed milk

For the white chocolate topping
50g (2oz) white chocolate, broken into pieces
150g (5oz) low-fat cream cheese
2 tbsp icing sugar, plus more to decorate
200g (7oz) mixed raspberries, blueberries and redcurrants, for decorating
white chocolate curls, to decorate

Preheat the oven to 200°C/fan 180°C/gas mark 6, and line a cupcake tin with paper cases.

Put all the cake ingredients in a large mixing bowl and beat for 2–3 minutes, ideally using an electric hand whisk, until pale and fluffy.

Divide the mixture between the paper cases and bake for 18–20 minutes, or until a skewer inserted into the centre of a cupcake comes out clean. Leave to cool in the tin for 5 minutes and then turn the cupcakes out on a wire rack and allow to cool completely.

To make the White Chocolate Topping: Put the white chocolate in a large heatproof bowl and place over a saucepan of barely simmering water, making sure the bowl does not touch the surface of the water. Heat until completely melted. Allow to cool slightly, then beat in the cream cheese and icing sugar until smooth. Chill in the refrigerator until it firms up a little.

Using a small palette knife or piping bag, cover the cupcakes with the topping. Decorate with the berries, dust with icing sugar and top with white chocolate curls.

FAT-FREE JASMINE & VIOLET CUPCAKES

Yes, it is possible – these dainty cupcakes are fat-free and delicious, too. The crystallized flowers give them a perfect look for a chic afternoon treat.

MAKES 12 CUPCAKES

For the crystallized flowers
a few violet and jasmine flowers
1 egg white, lightly beaten
2 tbsp granulated sugar

3 eggs
75g (3oz) golden caster sugar
75g (3oz) self-raising flour
1 tsp vanilla extract
2 drops of vanilla essence

For the jasmine drizzle
1 jasmine tea bag
3 tbsp boiling water
250g (8oz) icing sugar

First make the crystallized edible flowers: Dip the violet and jasmine flowers in the beaten egg white, then sprinkle them all over with granulated sugar. Leave them to dry on greaseproof paper overnight.

Preheat the oven to 200°C/fan 180°C/gas mark 6, and line a cupcake tin with paper cases.

In a large bowl whisk the eggs and sugar together until light, fluffy and doubled in volume, using an electric hand whisk. Sift the flour and gently fold it into the mixture, followed by the vanilla extract and essence.

Divide the mixture between the paper cases and bake for 20 minutes, or until a skewer inserted into a cupcake comes out clean. Leave to cool in the tin for 5 minutes, then transfer to a wire rack and allow to cool completely.

To make the Jasmine Drizzle: Put the tea bag in a small heatproof bowl and pour the boiling water over it. Leave to infuse until the tea is nice and strong, then remove the tea bag. Mix the icing sugar into the tea until you get a nice thick drizzling consistency. Drizzle over the cooled cupcakes and, before it sets, decorate with the crystallized violets and jasmine flowers.

GLUTEN-FREE PEAR & ALMOND CUPCAKES

These cupcakes are based on my favourite French pear dessert, Tarte Bordaloue. There is, of course, no pastry in this version and, being gluten-free, it is perfect for anyone with a gluten allergy.

MAKES 12 CUPCAKES

300g (10oz) ground almonds
1 tbsp gluten-free baking powder
100g (3½oz) caster sugar
100g (3½oz) butter, melted
2 eggs, beaten
250ml (8fl oz) milk
3 canned baby pears, drained
25g (1oz) flaked almonds
icing sugar, to decorate

For the poached pears
2 large ripe pears, peeled, cored
  and quartered
100g (3½oz) caster sugar
200ml (7fl oz) water
1 vanilla pod, split lengthways

If time allows poach the pears the day before: Put the sugar, water and vanilla pod in a saucepan. Slowly bring to the boil, stirring, until the sugar has dissolved. Add the pear quarters, cover and simmer over a low heat for 15 minutes. Leave to cool.

When you are ready to cook the cupcakes, preheat the oven to 200°C/fan 180°C/gas mark 6, and line a cupcake tin with paper cases.

In a large bowl, mix together the ground almonds, baking powder and sugar. Add the melted butter, eggs and milk, and mix until creamy. Drain the poached pears and cut them into small cubes, then fold these into the mixture.

Divide the mixture between the paper cases. Chop each of the canned baby pears into quarters (you should have 12 pieces) and place one quarter upright standing proud on top of each cake. Sprinkle over the flaked almonds and bake for 25–30 minutes, or until a skewer inserted into the centre of a cupcake comes out clean. Leave to cool in the tin for 5 minutes, then transfer to a wire rack and allow to cool completely. Dust with icing sugar before serving.

GRANOLA & MIXED SPICE CUPCAKES

These energy-packed cupcakes are perfect for kids' lunch boxes or for a healthy treat or snack to help keep you going through the day.

MAKES 12 CUPCAKES

225g (7½oz) wholemeal flour
100g (3½oz) granola, plus an extra 75g (3oz) for the topping
2 tsp baking powder
1 tsp mixed spice
1 tbsp poppy seeds
150g (5oz) dried apricots, chopped
50g (2oz) golden sultanas
3 tbsp sunflower oil
2 eggs
175ml (6fl oz) milk
100ml (3½oz) clear honey

Preheat the oven to 200°C/fan 180°C/gas mark 6, and line a cupcake tin with paper cases.

In a large mixing bowl, mix together the flour, 100g (3½oz) of granola, the baking powder, mixed spice, poppy seeds and dried fruit.

In another bowl, whisk together the oil, eggs, milk and honey until well blended. Pour into the dry ingredients and quickly stir.

Divide between the paper cases and sprinkle over the remaining granola. Bake for 25 minutes, or until a skewer inserted into a cupcake comes out clean. Leave to cool in the tin for 5 minutes, then transfer to a wire rack and allow to cool completely.

They will keep in the fridge for 2–3 days, or can be frozen.

GLUTEN-FREE PROVENÇAL ORANGE CUPCAKES

These flour-free cupcakes are perfect for people who have a gluten allergy. The decadent addition of ground almonds make these little cakes very moist, and the final drizzle of spicy syrup gives them a great tasty touch.

MAKES 12 CUPCAKES

175g (6oz) ground almonds
150g (5oz) caster sugar
2 tsp gluten-free baking powder
4 eggs, beaten
200ml (7fl oz) sunflower oil
finely grated zest of 1 lemon
finely grated zest of 2 oranges,
    ideally Seville, plus a few extra
    strands to decorate

For the syrup
juice of 1 lemon
juice of 2 oranges, ideally Seville
100g (3½oz) caster sugar
pinch of ground cloves
2 tsp ground cinnamon

Preheat the oven to 200°C/fan 180°C/gas mark 6, and line a cupcake tin with paper cases.

In a mixing bowl, combine the ground almonds, caster sugar and baking powder. Add the eggs and oil, and mix gently together. Stir the lemon and orange zest into the mixture.

Divide the mixture between the paper cases and bake for 30 minutes, or until a skewer inserted into the centre of a cupcake comes out clean. Leave to cool in the tin for 5 minutes, then transfer to a wire rack and allow to cool slightly.

To make the syrup: Pour the lemon and orange juices into a small saucepan. Add the sugar, cloves and cinnamon. Bring to the boil, then reduce the heat and simmer for 3 minutes.

Once the cupcakes have cooked but whilst still warm, pierce their tops several times with a cocktail stick. Spoon the syrup over the cakes and allow it to soak in whilst they cool. Decorate with strands of orange zest to finish.

COURGETTE CUPCAKES

These breakfast cupcakes make a tasty and nourishing kick-start to any day. I like to eat mine straight from the oven with honey, as you then get all the hearty flavour.

MAKES 12 CUPCAKES

250g (8oz) wholemeal flour
2 tsp baking powder
1 tsp mixed spices
100g (3½oz) mixed seeds
  (such as pumpkin, sesame,
  sunflower)
2 eggs
200ml (7fl oz) milk
4 tsp vegetable oil
4 tsp clear honey
150g (5oz) courgettes, grated
clear honey and Greek-style
  yoghurt, to serve (optional)

Preheat the oven to 200°C/fan 180°C/gas mark 6, and line a cupcake tin with paper cases.

In a large mixing bowl, thoroughly mix together all the dry ingredients (but do not sift the flour, as we want to keep all the goodness from the wholemeal). Add all the liquid ingredients and mix until nice and smooth. Fold in the courgette, taking care not to break it up.

Divide the mixture between the paper cases and bake for 25 minutes or until a skewer inserted into a cupcake comes out clean. Leave to cool in the tin for 5 minutes, then transfer to a wire rack and allow to cool completely.

To serve, drizzle with clear honey and some yoghurt if liked.

STYLING
CUPCAKES

VANILLA BUTTERCREAM FROSTING

This frosting can be tinted by using natural food colouring. I prefer to use an edible paste colouring rather than a liquid, as it doesn't affect the consistency of the frosting.

FOR 12 CUPCAKES

250g (8oz) unsalted butter, softened
600g (1lb 3oz) icing sugar
2 tbsp milk
1 tsp vanilla extract

In a large bowl, cream the butter, ideally using an electric hand whisk on medium speed. Blend in the sugar, a quarter of it at a time, beating well after each addition. Beat in the milk and vanilla extract, and continue mixing until light and fluffy.

Keep the frosting covered until you are ready to use it.

Using a small palette knife, smooth the frosting over the cupcakes. You can also create small spikes by quickly touching the frosting with the flat blade of the palette knife.

CREAM CHEESE FROSTING

Be careful when melting white chocolate, as it is much more temperamental than dark.

FOR 12 CUPCAKES

50g (2oz) white chocolate, broken into pieces
200g (7oz) cream cheese, softened
100g (3½oz) unsalted butter, softened
1 tsp vanilla extract
500g (1lb) icing sugar

Put the chocolate pieces in a heatproof bowl and place over a saucepan of barely simmering water making sure the bowl does not touch the surface of the water. Stir until the chocolate melts and is smooth. Allow to cool to room temperature.

In a bowl, using a wooden spoon or electric hand whisk, beat together the cream cheese and butter until smooth. Mix in the melted white chocolate and the vanilla extract. Gradually beat in the icing sugar until the mixture is fluffy.

Using a small palette knife, smooth the frosting over the cupcakes. You can also create small spikes by quickly touching the frosting with the flat blade of the palette knife.

ROYAL ICING

Use British Lion Standard egg whites. If you are worried about using raw eggs, you can buy reconstituted albumen powder instead.

**MAKES 500G
(1LB 2OZ)**

2 egg whites
1 tsp lemon juice
about 500g (1lb 2oz) icing sugar,
    sifted
edible food colouring paste
    (see page 127 for stockists)

Tip the egg whites into a bowl and stir in the lemon juice. Gradually add the sieved icing sugar, mixing well after each addition.

Continue adding small amounts of icing sugar until you achieve the desired consistency. For piping, the icing should be fairly stiff.

Edible food colouring paste is highly concentrated so only use a tiny amount. Dip a cocktail stick into the colouring paste. Mix well before adding more colouring paste to avoid streaks.

CHOCOLATE FROSTING

Use good-quality dark chocolate to make this rich chocolate buttercream frosting.
A great topping for any chocolate cupcakes or cakes.

FOR 12 CUPCAKES

200ml (7fl oz) single cream
250g (8oz) dark chocolate,
  finely chopped
50g (2oz) unsalted butter,
  softened

Heat the cream in a small saucepan, but do not allow it to boil.

Put the chocolate in a heatproof bowl and pour the hot cream over it through a fine sieve. Gently stir the cream into the chocolate until the mixture is nice and glossy. Gently mix in the soft butter. Leave to cool completely.

Once it is cool, ideally using an electric hand whisk, beat until nice and fluffy.

Use to fill or top cupcakes or cakes. You can use this without the final whipping to give a dark glossy chocolate coating.

VALENTINE'S DAY ROSE CUPCAKES

FOR 12 MINI CUPCAKES

You will need:
rose mould, approximately
   the same diameter as your
   cupcakes (see page 127
   for stockists)
cornflour, for dusting
chocolate paste or 'plastic',
   coloured with red and pink
   edible food colouring paste
   (see page 159 for stockists)
small paintbrush
boiled water, cooled
edible glitter in 'disco red' and
   'plum perfection' (see page 127
   for stockists)
piping bag with small star-tipped
   nozzle
½ quantity Vanilla Buttercream
   or Cream Cheese Frosting
   (see pages 84–5), coloured
   with red or pink edible food
   colouring pastes
12 mini cupcakes

1. Dust the inside of the mould with a little cornflour to stop the chocolate 'plastic' from sticking. Dab your fingertips into the cornflour, take a small ball of chocolate 'plastic' and press tightly into the mould.

2. Pop out the rose shape – it will not set hard so there is no need to leave it to dry.

3. Using a small dry paintbrush, brush off the excess cornflour from the rose shapes, then lightly brush the surface with the cooled boiled water.

4. Sprinkle red or pink glitter over, shake off the excess, and leave to dry. Using a piping bag with a star-tipped nozzle, pipe spirals of frosting on to each cupcake and top with a rose. Repeat for the remaining cupcakes

BUNNY CUPCAKES

FOR 12 CUPCAKES

You will need:
cornflour, for dusting
small rolling pin
50g (2oz) white ready-made
   sugar flower paste icing
   (see page 127 for stockists)
small dry paintbrush
edible rainbow dust in
   'Christmas red' (see page 127
   for stockists)
boiled water, cooled
100g (3½oz) desiccated coconut
small palette knife
1 quantity Vanilla Buttercream
   or Cream Cheese Frosting
   (see pages 84–5), coloured
   with green edible food
   colouring paste
12 chocolate or vanilla cupcake
   bases (see pages 14 and 62)

1. Dust a little cornflour over your work surface and roll out the petal
paste icing very thinly, about 2mm ⅛ inch) thick. Cut out 24 petal
shapes for ears, each 8cm (3½ inches) long and 2cm (¾ inch) at the
widest part (you may want to make a paper template to cut around).
Leave to dry in the refrigerator for several hours or overnight, until hard.

2. Using a small dry paintbrush, stain one side of each ear with red
edible rainbow dust, leaving a white border.

3. Lightly paint the white areas only of each ear on both sides with
cooled boiled water and immediately dip into the desiccated coconut
to coat. Leave to dry for a few minutes.

4. Using a small palette knife, spread the frosting over each cake.
Create a spiky grass effect by tapping the flat blade of the palette
knife on to the frosting. Poke 2 ears into each cake to finish.

CROWN CUPCAKES

1. Dust a little cornflour over your work surface to stop the icing from sticking, and roll out the sugar flower paste 5mm (¼inch) thick. Cut 12 strips, each 15cm (6 inches) long and 1cm (½inch) wide. Press the two ends together to make a circle, and leave to dry in the refrigerator for several hours or ideally overnight until hard.

2. Make a mini piping bag with the greaseproof paper by rolling it into a cone and folding the edges over. Fill with royal icing and snip off the tip so the icing flows. Pipe a row of small dots on top of the rim of the crown, holding the bag vertically with the tip close to the surface, squeeze a little icing out then pushing down and up sharply to finish. Pipe a second row of dots on top of the first row in between the gaps, then more dots to build up the tips of the crown. Leave to dry for a few minutes.

3. Lightly brush all over with the cooled boiled water and sprinkle with gold edible glitter. Use a small paintbrush to paint on additional colours as desired. Using a small palette knife, spread the frosting on top of each cake. (If your frosting seems a little too thick, dip your palette knife in hot water and this will make spreading easier.) Top with a glittering crown.

FOR 12 CUPCAKES

You will need:
cornflour, for dusting
small rolling pin
40g (1½oz) white ready-made
  sugar flower paste icing (see
  page 127 for stockists)
15cm (6-inch) square of
  greaseproof paper
50g (2oz) Royal Icing (see page 86)
small paintbrush
boiled water, cooled
edible glitter in gold, blue and red
  (see page 127 for stockists)
small palette knife
1 quantity Vanilla Buttercream
  or Cream Cheese Frosting
  (see pages 84–5), coloured
  with violet edible food colouring
  paste (see page 127 for stockists)
12 chocolate or vanilla cupcake
  bases (see pages 14 and 62)

BLING CUPCAKES

FOR 12 CUPCAKES

You will need:

1 quantity Vanilla Buttercream or Cream Cheese Frosting (see pages 84–5), coloured with peach edible food colouring paste

piping bag with a plain round nozzle

12 chocolate or vanilla cupcake bases (see pages 14 and 62)

edible diamonds, edible gold balls, sugar flowers, to decorate

tweezers

1. Your frosting needs to be free-flowing and not too stiff for this decoration. Fill the piping bag with frosting, twist the end tightly and squeeze gently until the frosting starts to come through. Starting at the rim furthest away from you, hold the piping bag at a 45° angle, pipe a dot and stop squeezing, tipping the bag vertically towards the centre of the cake.

2. Repeat around three-quarters of the rim, then create a second row in between the gaps, and keep repeating until you reach the middle.

3. Continue piping dots down the back of the cupcake to the rim. Repeat for the remaining cupcakes.

4. Use tweezers to arrange your chosen bling decorations carefully on top.

HEDGEHOG CUPCAKES

FOR 12 CUPCAKES

You will need:

15cm (6 inch) square of
  greaseproof paper

½ quantity Vanilla Buttercream
  or Cream Cheese Frosting,
  (see pages 84–5), 25g (1oz) left
  white (for the nose), half the
  remainder coloured with beige
  edible food paste and the rest
  coloured brown

12 chocolate or vanilla cupcake
  bases (see pages 14 and 62)

2 piping bags with plain round
  nozzles

24 chocolate 'eyes' (see page 127
  for stockists)

6 mini marshmallows

1. Make a mini piping bag with the greaseproof
paper by rolling it into a cone shape and folding
the edges over. Fill with the white frosting and
snip off the tip of the bag so the icing flows out.
First, make the base of the nose by piping a 2cm
(¾-inch) spiral of white frosting above the rim on
each cupcake.

2. Fill one of the nozzled piping bags with beige-coloured frosting and the other with brown-coloured frosting, twist the ends tightly and squeeze gently until the frosting starts to come through. Take the beige piping bag, hold at a 45° angle and pipe outwards around half the rim of a cupcake, squeezing a little and tilting the bag upright to form the spikes.

3. Now take the brown frosting and pipe more spikes overlapping the beige spikes to form a second row. Repeat, alternating the colours to cover the cake until you reach the nose.

4. Position the chocolate 'eyes' into position above the nose.

5. Cut the corner off a mini marshmallow and place on top of the white frosting to form the tip of the nose. Repeat with the remaining cupcakes.

SUMMER FLOWER CUPCAKES

FOR 12 CUPCAKES

You will need:
small palette knife
1 quantity Vanilla Buttercream
or Cream Cheese frosting
(see pages 84–5), coloured
with violet edible food
colouring paste
12 chocolate or vanilla cupcake
bases (see pages 14 and 62)
piping bag with a plain nozzle
(about 5mm/¼ inch)
½ quantity Vanilla Buttercream
or Cream Cheese Frosting,
25g (1oz) coloured with black
edible food colouring paste
(for the stigma), the remainder
coloured with orange edible
food colouring paste
15cm (6-inch) square of
greaseproof paper

1. Using a small palette knife, spread the violet-coloured frosting over each cupcake to cover.

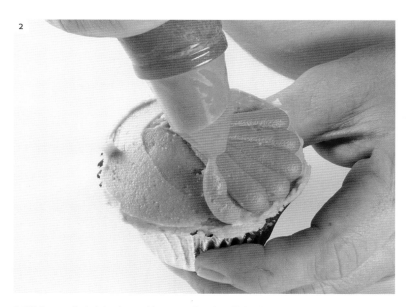

2

2. Fill the nozzled piping bag with orange frosting. Twist the end
tightly and squeeze gently until the frosting starts to come through.
Holding the bag at a 45° angle, start at the rim and pipe a petal shape
by squeezing the bag across the cake towards the centre and twist
upwards to finish. Repeat around the cake to cover.

3. Repeat a second layer over the top of first layer.

4. Make a mini piping bag with the greaseproof paper by rolling it into a cone shape and folding the edges over. Fill with black frosting and snip off the tip of the bag so the icing flows out. Pipe small dots in the centre of the cupcake to form the stigma, piling them to build up some height. Repeat with the remaining cupcakes.

POKE-IN-THE-EYE CUPCAKES

FOR 12 CUPCAKES

You will need:
100g (3½oz) white chocolate
12 dome-shaped chocolates
   (such as Lindor)
small paintbrush
edible rainbow dust in red
   (see page 127 for stockists)
boiled water, cooled
edible glitter in blue, green
   and black (see page 127 for
   stockists)
1 quantity Vanilla Buttercream
   or Cream Cheese Frosting
   (see pages 84–5), coloured
   with edible colouring pastes
12 chocolate or vanilla cupcake
   bases (see pages 14 and 62)
15cm (6-inch) square of
   greaseproof paper
piping gel, coloured with red
   edible colouring paste

1. Melt the white chocolate in a heatproof bowl placed over a saucepan of barely simmering water, making sure the bowl does not touch the surface of the water. Dip the chocolates in the white chocolate until completely covered and leave to set on a plate in the refrigerator for 2 hours.

2. Using a small dry paintbrush, dust red edible rainbow dust over the white chocolate eyeballs.

3. Lightly brush a circle of water on one side, then paint a ring using edible blue and green glitter. Paint the centre with black edible glitter.

4. Using the tip of a small sharp knife, score from the centre of the eyeball outwards several times to create a veined effect. Spread frosting over the cupcakes and place an eyeball on top.

5. Make a mini piping bag with the greaseproof paper by rolling into a cone shape and folding the edges over. Fill with red piping gel and snip off the tip of the bag so the icing flows out. Pipe the gel into the centre of the eyeball and let it drizzle down over the frosting. Repeat with the remaining cupcakes.

CHOCOLATE HONEYCOMB CUPCAKES

FOR 12 CUPCAKES

You will need:
6 pieces of bubble wrap,
  each 10 x 20cm (4 x 8 inches)
200g (7oz) dark, milk or white
  chocolate, melted
1 quantity Vanilla Buttercream
  or Cream Cheese Frosting
  (see pages 84–5)
12 chocolate cupcake bases
  (see page 14)
small paintbrush with soft bristles
edible rainbow dust in gold (see
  page 127 for stockists)
edible glitter in gold (optional)

1. Wash and dry the bubble wrap and place on plates (or any flat surface that will fit in your refrigerator) with the bubbles face up. Pour the melted chocolate over the bubble wrap, dividing the chocolate equally between each piece.

2. Use a knife to spread the chocolate out, then leave to set in the refrigerator for 1 hour. Meanwhile, spread frosting on top of each cupcake.

3. Once the chocolate has set, carefully peel off and discard the bubble wrap.

4. Use a small dry paintbrush to highlight areas of the chocolate honeycomb with gold edible rainbow dust.

5. Then snap each chocolate piece into 4 so you have 24 pieces. Push 2 pieces into each cupcake and sprinkle a pinch of edible glitter down the sides of the frosting to finish.

SNOWFLAKE CUPCAKES

FOR 12 CUPCAKES

You will need:
cornflour, for dusting
small rolling pin
40g (1½oz) white ready-made
    sugar flower paste icing
snowflake cutter (see page 127
    for stockists)
small paintbrush with soft bristles
boiled water, cooled
edible glitter in silver (see page
    127 for stockists)
piping bag with a plain nozzle
1 quantity Vanilla Buttercream
    or Cream Cheese Frosting (see
    pages 84–5), coloured with red
    edible food colouring paste
12 chocolate or vanilla cupcake
    bases (see pages 14 and 62)

1. Dust a little cornflour over your work surface
to stop the icing from sticking, and roll out the
sugar flower paste icing very thinly, about 2mm
(¹/8 inch) thick.

2. Using a snowflake cutter, cut out 12 shapes and leave to dry in the refrigerator for several hours or ideally overnight, until hard.

3. Using a small paintbrush, lightly brush cooled boiled water over the surface of the snowflake. Cover with edible glitter and shake off the excess, then leave to dry for a few minutes.

4. Fill the piping bag with frosting, twist the end tightly and squeeze gently until the frosting starts to come through. Hold the bag vertically and slowly pipe a ring of icing around the edge of a cupcake, then continue in a spiral until you reach the centre and the cupcake is covered. Stop the pressure, then push the bag down and up sharply to finish.

5. Repeat for the remaining cupcakes and position a snowflake on top of each cupcake.

CHRISTMAS TREE BAUBLE CUPCAKES

FOR 12 CUPCAKES

You will need:
bauble mould (see page 127 for
  stockists)
cornflour, for dusting
40g (1½oz) white ready-made
  sugar flower paste icing
small paintbrush
edible rainbow dust in gold
  (see page 127 for stockists)
boiled water, cooled
edible glitter in gold (see page 159
  for stockists)
piping bag with 5mm (¼ inch)
  plain nozzle
1 quantity Vanilla Buttercream
  or Cream Cheese Frosting
  (see pages 84–5), coloured
  with green edible food
  colouring paste
12 chocolate or vanilla cupcake
  bases (see pages 14 and 62)

1. Dust the inside of the mould with a little
cornflour. Dab your fingertips into the cornflour
to stop them sticking and take a small ball of
sugar flower paste icing and press it tightly into
the bauble mould. Pop out the shape and repeat
until you have 12 baubles.

2. Using a small dry paintbrush, brush the excess cornflour off the bauble shapes, then leave to set in the refrigerator until hard for a few hours or ideally overnight.

3. Once set, use a small paintbrush to paint the top of the attaching piece with gold coloured edible rainbow dust. Then lightly brush the bauble base (but not the attachment top) with the cooled boiled water.

4. Sprinkle edible glitter over the bauble, shake off the excess and leave to dry.

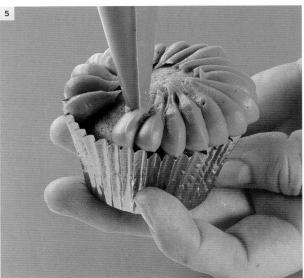

5. To create the Christmas tree effect, the frosting needs to be free-flowing and not too stiff. Fill the piping bag with frosting, twist the end tightly and squeeze gently until the frosting starts to come through. Pipe a dot on the rim of the cupcake, stop squeezing, tip the bag vertically and push the tip of the nozzle towards the centre of the cake. Repeat around the rim, then create a second row in between the gaps and repeat until you reach the middle. Pipe a swirl on top to finish and place a bauble on top.

HOLLY LEAF CUPCAKES

FOR 12 CUPCAKES

You will need:
cornflour, for dusting
small rolling pin
50g (2oz) green ready-made
   sugar flower paste icing (see
   page 127 for stockists)
small sharp knife
small paintbrush with soft
   bristles
boiled water, cooled
edible glitter in 'disco green',
   'yellow' and 'super nova purple'
   (see page 127 for stockists)
piping bag with a 5mm (¼ inch
   plain nozzle
1 quantity Vanilla Buttercream
   or Cream Cheese Frosting
   (see pages 84–5), coloured
   with red, green and/or yellow
   edible food colouring pastes
12 chocolate or vanilla cupcake
   bases (see pages 14 and 62)

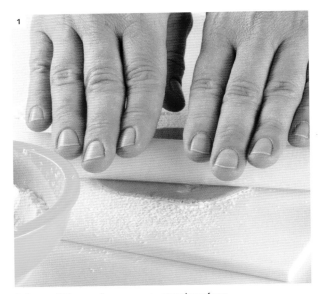

1. Dust a little cornflour over your work surface
to stop the icing from sticking, and roll out the
sugar flower paste icing very thinly, about 2mm
(¹/₈ inch) thick.

2. Using the tip of a small sharp knife, carefully cut out 12 holly leaf shapes. (You may find it easier to make a paper template first to cut round.) Leave to dry in the refrigerator for several hours or ideally overnight, until hard.

3. Using a small paintbrush, lightly brush cooled boiled water over the surface of the holly leaves. Cover with edible glitter and shake off the excess, then leave to dry for a few minutes.

4. Fill the piping bag with frosting, twist the end tightly and squeeze gently until the frosting starts to come through. Hold the bag vertically and slowly pipe a ring of icing around the edge of a cupcake, then continue in a spiral until you reach the centre and the cupcake is covered. Stop the pressure, then push the bag down and up sharply to finish.

5. Poke the holly leaf into the top of each cupcake to finish. Repeat with the remaining cupcakes.

INDEX

USEFUL CONTACTS

**Blue Ribbons
Sugarcraft Centre**
www.blueribbons.co.uk
Tel. +44 (0)20 8941 1591

Stockist of rose-shaped silicone rubber push moulds; edible food colouring pastes; edible rainbow dust and glitter; edible confectioners' glaze and sugar decorations including diamonds and flowers.

Cake Craft Shop
www.cakecraftshop.co.uk
Tel. +44 (0)1732 463573

Stockist of edible food colouring pastes; edible glaze spray and sugar decorations and flowers.

FPC Sugarcraft
www.fpcsugarcraft.co.uk
Tel. +44 (0)117 9853249

Online store selling a large selection of silicone rubber moulds, including rose and Christmas tree bauble shapes.

**Jane Asher
Party Cakes & Sugarcraft**
www.janeasher.com
Tel. +44 (0)20 7584 6177

Shop and online store selling edible food colouring pastes; edible rainbow dust and glitters; flavourings; sugar flower paste and ready-made icings; confectioners' glaze; piping gel; edible gold leaf and decorations.

Squires Kitchen
www.squires-shop.com
Tel. +44 (0)1252 260260

Shop and online store selling silicone rubber push moulds; snowflake, flower and holly leaf-shaped plunger cutters; chocolate paste; sugar flower paste and ready-made icings; edible gold leaf and edible confectioners' glaze.

Sugar Shack
www.sugarshack.co.uk
Tel. +44 (0)20 8204 2994

Shop and online store selling edible rainbow dust and glitters; flavourings; sugar flower paste and ready-made icings; confectioners' glaze; piping gel and edible decorations.

Totally Sugar Crafts
www.totallysugarcrafts.co.uk/
Tel. +44 (0)1733 700 374

Online store selling snowflake plunger cutters; edible food colouring pastes and edible rainbow dust and glitters.

ABOUT THE AUTHORS

Eric Lanlard, master pâtissier and twice winner of the prestigious Continental Pâtissier of the Year at The British Baking Awards, has earned himself an international reputation for superlative cakes with an impressive A-list clientele.

Having trained in France, Eric moved to London where he ran the pâtisserie business for Albert and Michel Roux. He stayed there for five years before launching his own business, and now creates cakes for his private clients at his cake emporium Cake Boy.

Eric is an experienced TV presenter with two series of *Glamour Puds* to his name. He has also appeared on numerous TV food shows including *The Taste Masterchef: The Professionals* and *Market Kitchen*. He has also presented two series' of *Baking Mad with Eric Lanlard* for Channel 4.

He is author of *Chocolat*, *Tart It Up!*, *Home Bake* (Mitchell Beazley) and *Master Cakes* (Hamlyn) and runs regular classes at his London cookery school.

Canadian-born **Patrick Cox** relocated to London in 1983 and quickly made a mark with his footwear designs. Within a decade, his was the label on fashionable feet all over the world.

After 20 years in the shoe business he was ready for a sabbatical, and in 2010 he launched Soho baking venture Cox Cookies & Cake with Eric Lanlard.